MUSIC AND INSTRUMENTS
FOR CHILDREN TO MAKE

Music Involvement Series   Book One

By JOHN HAWKINSON and MARTHA FAULHABER

MUSIC AND INSTRUMENTS FOR CHILDREN TO MAKE

Illustrated by JOHN HAWKINSON

ALBERT WHITMAN & Company, Chicago

Art Books by
John Hawkinson

COLLECT, PRINT AND PAINT FROM NATURE
MORE TO COLLECT AND PAINT FROM NATURE
OUR WONDERFUL WAYSIDE
PASTELS ARE GREAT!

Music Involvement Series
Book Two
RHYTHMS, MUSIC AND INSTRUMENTS TO MAKE

Standard Book Number 8075-5351-4
©Copyright by Albert Whitman & Company, Chicago
Library of Congress Card Number 70-79543
Published simultaneously in Canada by
George J. McLeod, Ltd., Toronto
Lithographed in the United States of America

HOW PARENTS AND TEACHERS
CAN USE THIS BOOK WITH CHILDREN

There are many books about music for children, but there are few books for children about music. The distinction is a real one and reflects two different approaches to children and to music.

This book, *Music and Instruments for Children to Make,* is for the child, for him to read independently or with help. It is filled with musical experiences that lead to discoveries about music and its possibilities. The purpose of this book, then, is not to teach music to the young child; it is to let him find music as he becomes aware of his own everyday experiences with rhythm and sound, the materials of music.

Where does learning about music begin? Natural rhythmic movements, such as walking and running, are the basis for discovering rhythm. The child experiments with his voice, making high and low sounds, loud ones and soft ones. He listens to others who try out different sounds, and he learns something about voices and singing as he does so.

Children observe that sound can be produced in many ways. An empty box or can, as this book shows, becomes a drum, the simplest of musical instruments. A drum suggests many ways to use rhythms and singing. Then comes a box harp, a homemade stringed instrument, that can be used in a variety of ways. Finally there are instructions for a set of panpipes, made of materials that are easily assembled. With these three homemade instruments—drum, box harp, and panpipes—the child is ready to make music and to compose music of his own.

It is important to remember that children have been making music for thousands of years. They have not waited for complex notational systems and advanced adult instruments. They have used rhythmic body motions and the kind of instruments they can make for themselves. Our children of today can do this, too. They can discover rhythm and the beauty of their own voices and sounds around them. When girls and boys are aware of these basic elements, they are ready to explore ways of creating music.

A young child aware of rhythm and sound is naturally a composer or improviser. He learns music as he learns language, by using it. Learning is personal experience and keeps fresh a creative attitude that carries over to whatever level of music the individual may later pursue. It is this approach that we emphasize.

Here are a few suggestions for a parent who uses this book at home or a teacher who follows it in a classroom.

One of the first activities involves children in listening to the variety of sound around them. The bark of a dog, the sound of wind blowing through the trees, the thunder crashing, are examples.

A child must learn to be very quiet to be attentive to sounds. In the classroom, children can be asked to write down and describe what they hear, telling what seems different about certain sounds. Discussing what has been heard will help everyone become conscious of certain aspects of sound: sounds can be high or low; soft or loud; squeaky, full, hollow, and so on. Children can also listen for the rhythmic patterns created by repeated sounds.

Once there is consciousness of rhythm and sound, children begin to experiment with these for themselves. In a classroom, girls and boys can work in small groups to make the experiments with rhythm effective. For example, one small group can walk or march around the room while the other children imitate the walking rhythm by clapping. One child can run on tiptoes or skip while the rest of the children clap the rhythm. Be sure to let children bring in their own examples of rhythm and think of the book pages as a beginning, not a complete program.

For the experiments with sound the children can also divide into groups to explore contrasts such as high and low, soft and loud. Nursery rhymes are effective for this purpose. As they listen to music, children can be alert to notice contrasts.

When girls and boys experiment with their own voices they can all slide or step from their lowest sound to their highest. As they sing a song like "Are You Sleeping?" they can listen for the steps they are making with their voices.

A section of this book introduces children to musical instruments. There are directions for making drums and two other simple instruments. The box harp is an example of a stringed instrument, the panpipes an example of a blowing instrument. The adult should give the children as much freedom as possible to follow the simple directions. A teacher or parent can provide the space and materials, then guide only as necessary. The step-by-step procedures are carefully detailed. It will be helpful in making the panpipes if the adult checks to see that pipes are cut to exact measure and filled with clay to produce pitches accurate for everyone. But the educational value in letting children follow the directions and work by themselves cannot be overestimated.

When their instruments are finished, children can work out their own small groups and present a program with ideas from this book. An entire class can learn to play panpipes together. The excitement and creativity of making music shines through such experiences. Music involvement is a reality.

We hope that each parent and teacher and child who uses this book will expand and develop it in his own way. The only guide is one's own imagination and musical feeling.

Rhythms Around Us

Listen to the rhythm of a clock ticking.

Listen to the rhythm of your feet when you are walking.

Listen to the rhythm of falling rain.

Sounds Around Us

Listen to the sound
of a bird singing.

Listen to the sound
of dogs barking.

Listen to the sound of bells ringing.

You Can Make Rhythm . . .

As you walk   walk   walk

As you run   run   run   run   run   run

As you skip   a-skip   a-skip   a-skip

You Can Make Sound...

When you shout,

If you whisper,

When you sing your name,

Or hum a tune.

Rhythms to Clap

You can clap rhythms, too. Walk now and clap to your walk. Each time your foot takes a step, give a clap. Stop walking and keep on clapping.

Now count "**One**, Two, Three, Four" as you walk and give a loud clap every time you take a step on "**One**." This is the way you make a marching rhythm.

You can clap a running rhythm too. It is difficult to clap while you are running, but you can clap while a friend runs on tiptoes. He should step twice as fast as a walk to make his running rhythm.

Now try clapping a walking rhythm while someone runs. The two rhythms will fit together like this: One walk = Two runs.

  Walk   walk   walk   walk
run run   run run   run run   run run

Try clapping the skipping rhythm of your friends. Clap one long clap as they step and short clap as they hop.

skip

a –

skip

a –

Skip

a –

skip

Skip	a – skip	a – skip	a – skip
long	**short long**	**short long**	**short long**

You can find your walking and running rhythms in rhymes and songs.

Clap and say the rhyme:

Rain,	rain,	go	a – way,	come	a – gain	some	o – ther	day.
walk	**walk**	**run run walk**		**run**	**run run**	**run**	**run run**	**walk**

Try:

One,	two,	tie	my	shoe.	Three,	four,	shut	the	door.
walk	**walk**	**run**	**run**	**walk**	**walk**	**walk**	**run**	**run**	**walk**

Now clap the rhythm all by itself. Make other rhythms that use the walking and running clap. Clap to music you hear on the radio or television.

Rhythms for Drums

Try your rhythms on a drum. A coffee can with a plastic lid or an oatmeal box will make a good drum. Beat it with your hand or a pencil.

Beat your drum in rhythm with your walk. Make it sound like a march.

Tap a running rhythm on your drum. Make it sound like falling rain.

Tap a skipping rhythm on your drum.

More Rhythms for Drums

Tie or tape three different sized cans or boxes together to make bongo drums. Tap your name. Is it Rumpelstiltskin? What is it?

Be a drummer. Begin a rhythm of your very own. Have a friend dance to your rhythm. Make it slow. Make it fast.

Drumming to a Rhyme

Tap the rhythm of "Hot Cross Buns" on your drums as you say the rhyme.

Hot   cross   buns,   **wait**   **(Repeat)**

One   a   pen-ny,   two   a   pen-ny,

Hot   cross   buns.   **wait**

Can you tell that you are tapping a walking rhythm for "Hot Cross Buns"? There is a wait on the word "buns." Walk, walk, walk, **wait.** On "One a penny, two a penny" you tap a faster rhythm like your running rhythm. You have eight quick taps.

Other Rhythm Instruments

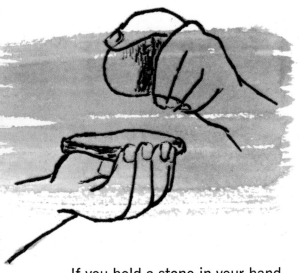

If you hold a stone in your hand, like this, and tap it with another stone, it will be a rhythm instrument.

Hold a stick in one hand and hit it with another stick. Try your different rhythms with your rhythm sticks.

Make a gong from a pot lid. Hit it on the side. Hit two lids together like cymbals. Sing "Pop Goes the Weasel" and crash the cymbals together on the word "pop."

Use two long blocks from a block set or scrap lumber and go clippity-clop with them on a table to make the rhythm of a galloping horse. You can also hold one block in your hand and tap it with a pencil or spoon.

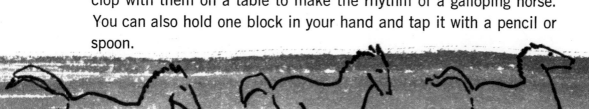

Fill small boxes or cans with a handful of rice or dried beans. Shake the boxes or cans like maracas to the rhythm of dance music.

Wherever you go, look for little bells that you can attach to a cord and use as a rhythm instrument.

Having Fun with Nursery Rhymes

Jack and Jill went up the hill
To fetch a pail of water.
Jack fell down
And broke his crown,
And Jill came tumbling after.

As you say the rhyme, tap its rhythm on your rhythm instruments. Save your maracas and gong for the line "Jack fell down." The maracas can give the effect of rolling down the hill, and the gong is sounded on the word "down."

Try your own ideas with other nursery rhymes.

Your Own Band

You can have a rhythm band with your friends using your rhythm instruments. Take turns being the conductor. Play rhymes or songs you know, such as "Are You Sleeping?" Think about what instruments you will want to use to wake up Brother John.

Listening to Sounds

Tap on a glass.

Tap on the floor.

Tap on a rug.

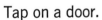

Tap on a door.

Tap on things all over the house.
What kind of sounds do you hear?
What sounds do you like best of all?

Loud and Soft Sounds

Sounds can be loud.
Listen to a dog bark.

Sounds can be soft.
Listen to a cat purr.

Tap on your drum.
Try to sound as
loud as thunder.
Try to sound as soft
as falling snow.
Tap from your softest
sound to your loudest
sound.

High and Low Sounds

Sounds can be high. Say "Who's been eating my porridge?" with your highest voice, like Baby Bear in "The Three Bears." Can you sing that high?

Sounds can be low. Now say "Who's been eating my porridge?" with your lowest voice, like Papa Bear. Can you sing that low?

Can you sing in a middle-sized voice, like Mama Bear?

Drop from your
highest sound
to your lowest
sound.

Sing your lowest sound.
Then slide from your
lowest to your highest sound.

When you have reached your highest sound, step down again.

Take small steps with your voice going from your lowest to your highest sound. Sing "Up, up, up" as you climb.

Can you hear the steps your voice makes when you sing "Hot Cross Buns"?

Listen to the way your voice steps when you sing "Are You Sleeping?" Raise your hand when your voice steps up and lower your hand when your voice steps down. Sometimes your voice will jump over a step or two. The words going up and down show how the tune goes up and down when you sing.

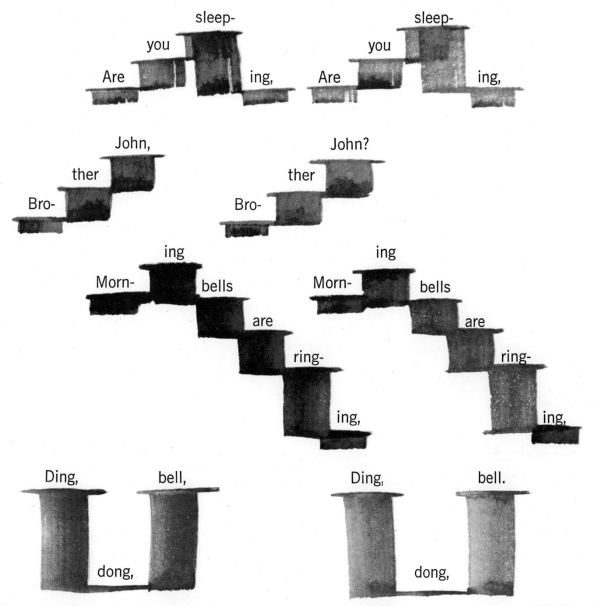

Making Sounds in Other Ways

There are other ways besides with the voice to make sound. The first man could only growl like a bear. That was his voice sound. But then he listened to the wind in the trees, the water running in the brook, and the birds singing all around him.

He made something to blow that sounded like a bird.

And he made something to pluck that sounded like the wind in the trees.

He beat on a hollow log, and his children sang and danced to the rhythms he made.

Today we have many kinds of instruments for playing music, and they give us many different sounds.

Oboe

Double flute

Cello

Drum

Trombone

Banjo

Guitar

Electric guitar

Recorder

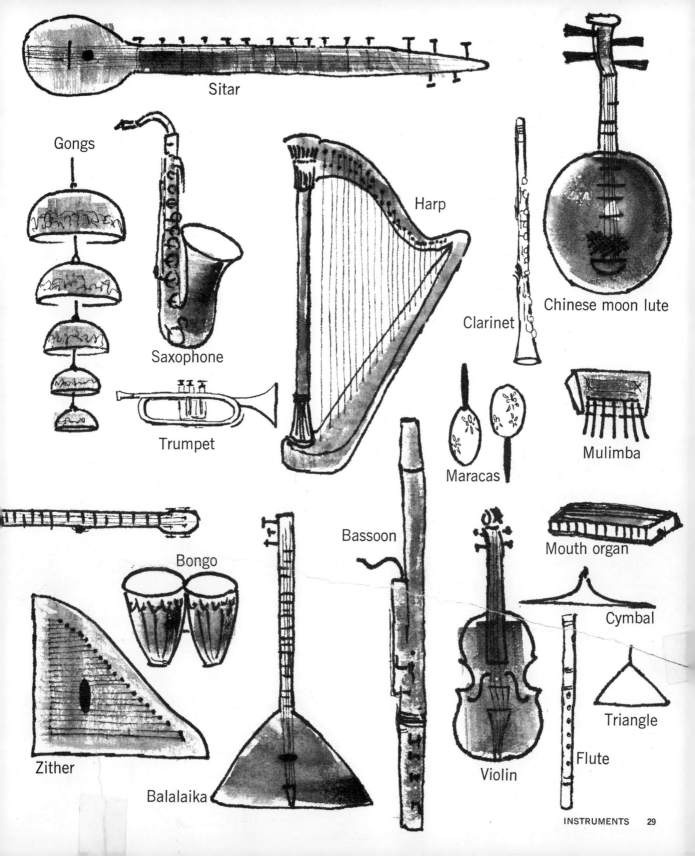

Sitar

Gongs

Saxophone

Trumpet

Harp

Clarinet

Chinese moon lute

Maracas

Mulimba

Zither

Bongo

Balalaika

Bassoon

Violin

Mouth organ

Cymbal

Flute

Triangle

Making Your Own Stringed Instrument, a Box Harp

Here is what you will need:
1. A cardboard box about 18 x 10 x 8 inches. You can get this free in a grocery store.
2. Monofilament fishing line, ten to twenty pound weight. Buy this where fishing equipment is sold. Button cord can be substituted.
3. A pencil.
4. Tape or glue.
5. Two popsicle sticks.
6. A ballpoint pen for punching holes.

Step 1
Glue or tape the box to close all its openings.

Step 2
With your old ballpoint pen, punch through the box, as shown. Cut a piece of fishline about twice as long as the box, put it through the two holes and tie securely.

Step 3
Turn the box around. At the other end, about two inches from the top, punch a hole. Wrap tape around the middle of a pencil and insert it in the hole.

Step 4

Next wrap the fishline around the pencil, pulling it tight so that the pencil is against the box. Tie the line or loop it around the pencil so that it won't slip.

Step 5

Push the pencil down until the point can be pushed up into the top of the box to hold the line taut.

If the line is not tight enough, remove the pencil and make a loop around it.

Step 6

Put a popsicle stick (or an old pencil) at each end under the fishline so that the stick rests on the edge of the box. Tape the stick down.

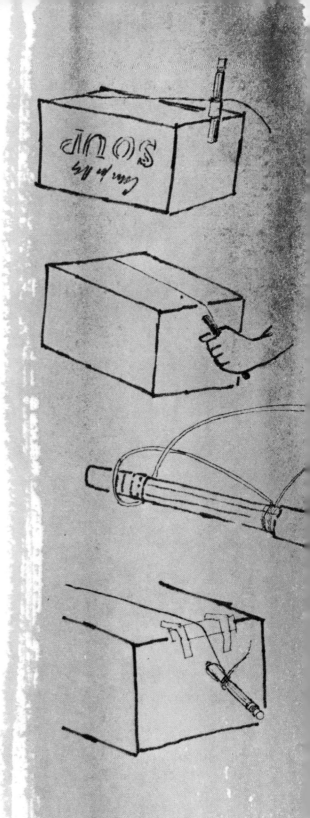

Step 7

Cut a piece of cardboard about an inch wide and three inches long. Score in two places with a blunt knife.

Fold and tape to make a "bridge." Make a small notch for the string to slide against. Place your bridge under the string, and you are ready to play your first stringed instrument.

Place the bridge about an inch away from the pencil end of the box. Pluck the string with your finger to make it hum. Listen to the sound and sing it. Now move the bridge toward the middle of the box to shorten the string. Pluck, listen, and sing this sound. Is it a higher sound? Keep plucking the string as you move the bridge along and listen carefully to the sound as you pluck.

Here are experiments like your voice experiments to try on the box harp. Place the bridge about two inches from the end opposite the pencil end of your box harp, as illustrated. Slide the bridge from this end to the pencil end as you pluck. When you do this, you are making what musicians call a "glissando."

Begin at the same end and see if you can make the sounds step down as you did with your voice. Move the bridge about half an inch at a time toward the pencil end. Move the bridge back again to hear the sounds go higher.

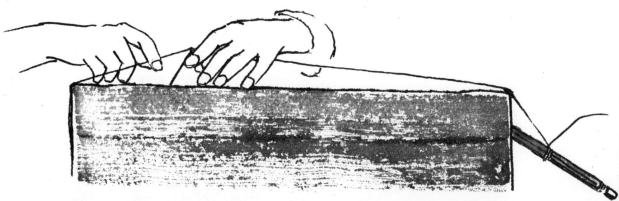

Pluck the rhythm of your name. Move your bridge until you find a sound or two that you like for your name. Sing your name to those sounds. Try the names of friends.

Pluck the rhythm of a rhyme—

> Rain, rain, go away,
> Come again another day.

Find a tune on your box harp to go with the rhyme. Can you think of a way to picture your tune?

Making a Dancing Tune

Find a drummer, and you can play together to make music for dancing. Match the drummer's rhythm on your box harp. Move your bridge back and forth as you pluck to make a dancing tune. Let the drummer change his rhythm to a running or skipping rhythm for a faster dance. Then try a slow rhythm or the rhythm of a rhyme. Once you have the idea, invent your own dance rhythms.

One a-jump,
Two a-jump,
Three a-jump,
Four!

Pick yourself
A partner
And then jump
Some more!

More Tunes

Have your drummer tap the rhythm of your jumping rhyme. Pluck your box harp in rhythm with the words of the rhyme as you say them. Move your bridge as you pluck to make a tune for your rhyme.

Instruments to Blow

Many musical instruments make a sound when you blow them.

Some instruments make a big deep sound. Some make a high sweet sound that is soft and mellow. Some sound high, while others sound low.

Some can sound loud and blaring, like a trumpet.

You can make a sound something like a trumpet's if you blow into a shower hose. Be sure to press your lips tightly together.

Children all over the world blow flutes—all kinds of flutes.

If you blow across the mouth of a bottle you can make a sound like one made by a flute.

Making Panpipes

Panpipes are the easiest kind of flute to make and tune. To make panpipes you will need:

1 Rubber shower hose, sold at a hardware store or a five-and-ten.
2 Modeling clay.
3 Masking tape.

Here are the tools you will need:
Ruler   Scissors   Pencil

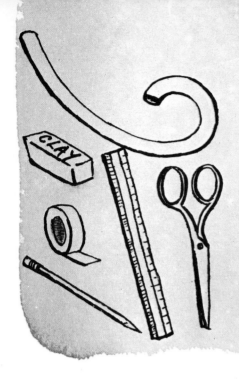

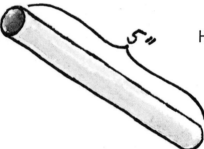

Here is what you do.

Step 1
With your scissors, cut off a piece of hose 5 inches long. If the hose has too much curve, straighten it by soaking it in hot water.

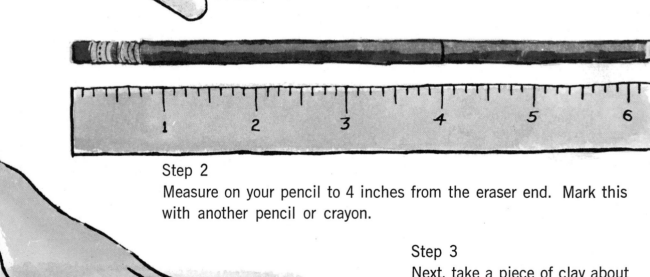

Step 2
Measure on your pencil to 4 inches from the eraser end. Mark this with another pencil or crayon.

Step 3
Next, take a piece of clay about the size of a marble and roll it into a cylinder shape about an inch long.

Step 4

Put the piece of clay into one end of the 5-inch piece of hose. Hold your finger over the clay. Put your marked pencil in the other end until it reaches the 4-inch mark. This will be the right length for the inside of your pipe. The clay should fit tightly so that you can't see through the pipe.

If there is too much clay, push it out with the pencil. If there is not enough, take out the pencil and drop in little pieces of clay. When the outside is just the length of your marked pencil, the pipe will give you a certain sound or pitch when you blow it. This pitch is named G in the musical world.

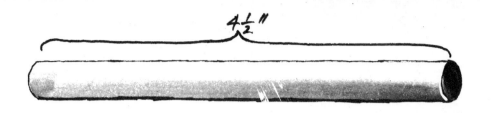

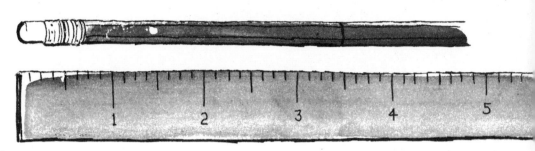

Step 5

Now you are ready to make the next pipe which will give you the sound (pitch) A. You make it as you made the other pipe. First cut 4½ inches of hose. Mark the pencil at 3½ inches for the inside of this pipe.

For the third pipe, cut your hose to 3¾ inches and mark your pencil at 3⅛ inches for the inside of the pipe. This will give you the sound (pitch) B.

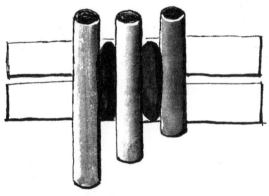

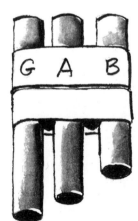

Step 6

Now put the pipes together. Place a little wad of clay between the pipes and then wrap them with tape. You have your own blowing instrument that gives you three different sounds. Mark each pipe with its pitch.

It may take a little time to learn to blow your panpipes. Here is a way to help you learn. Hold the pipes so that the shortest one is on your right. Press the open end of the shortest pipe against the top of your lower lip. Blow across the pipe. This is like blowing across the top of a bottle. Keep trying until you get a sound. Then blow the other two pipes.

Blow a loud sound. Blow a soft sound. Blow the highest sound and the lowest sound. Blow your name on the pipes.

With your panpipes you can play "Hot Cross Buns." First tap "Hot Cross Buns" on your drum as you sing. Then pick up your pipes and play as you see in the pictures.

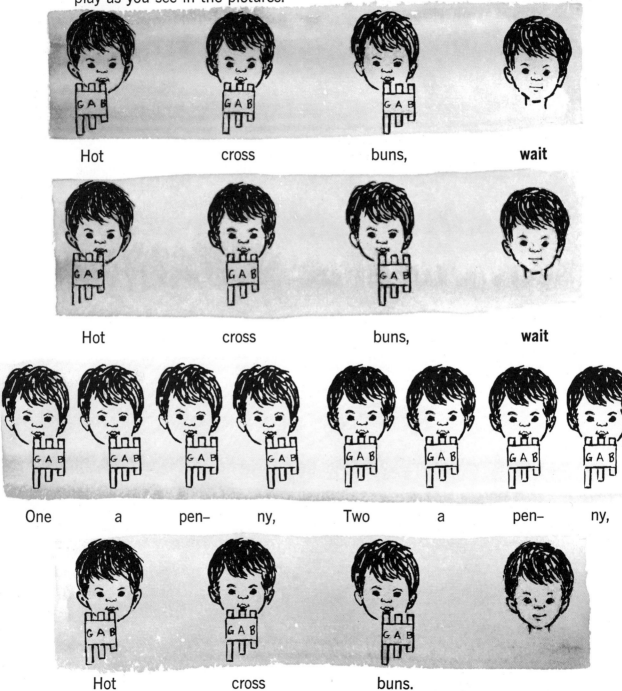

Hot cross buns, **wait**

Hot cross buns, **wait**

One a pen– ny, Two a pen– ny,

Hot cross buns.

Have a friend tap a marching rhythm on his drum. Play a tune that fits his rhythm. Begin with any pipe. Blow in any order. You have your own marching music.

Can you find the tune of "Mary Had a Little Lamb" on your pipes? It begins on B. Let the drummer keep the rhythm. Now go on to make up tunes of your own.

Fun with Street Calls

Have you ever heard the ice cream man calling? He rings a little bell and sings. You can play his song on your pipes. The letters above each word are the pipes you play to the rhythm of the words. Have a friend sing the song as you play.

B	B	B	A	G	A
Ice	cream,	ice	cream	for	sale,

A	A	A	A	A	A
Marsh–	mal–	low,	co –	co–	nut,

A	A	A
Pe –	can,	peach.

A	A	A	A	A
Cho–	co–	late,	ap–	ple,

A	A	B
Le –	mon,	lime.

B	A	A	A	A	A
Cran–	ber –	ry,	straw–	ber–	ry,

A	A	A	A	A	A
Rasp–	ber–	ry,	blue–	ber–	ry,

A	A	A	A	A	A	A
Goose–ber–	ry,	boy–	sen–	ber –	ry,	

A	A	A	A	A	A	A
Ap–	ple –ber–	ry,	eve –	ry–	ber–ry!	

A	G	A	B	A	G	A
Ice	cre – am,	ice	cream	for	sale!	

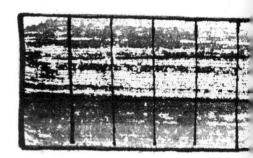

A Quiet Song

B	**B**	**B**	**A**	**A**	**B**
The	stars	are	bright	for	you,
B	**G**	**A**	**A**	**A**	**B**
Sleep,	my	lit –	tle	one,	sleep,
B	**A**	**B**	**A**	**G**	
The	night	is	so	still.	

Read the little poem. It is a lullaby. See if you can play a quiet melody on your panpipes to go with the words of the poem. The letters marked above the words are the pipes one child used for his song. When you have composed your own tune, let a friend play a rocking rhythm on the box harp.

A Gay Dance

This is a song for box harp, panpipes, and drum or other rhythm instruments. Let the drummer begin tapping like the ticking of a clock. This will give a steady rhythm or beat that will help all the players keep together. The box harp player and other rhythm players will play a second rhythm to the words of the dance poem given below. Say the words as you pluck or tap to help you keep the rhythm going. Your two rhythms will fit together like this:

Tick		**Tock**		**Tick**		**Tock**
Round	and	round	and	round	we	go,

Tick	**Tock**	**Tick**	**Tock**
Laughing,	dancing,	whirling,	twirling.

Tick	**Tock**	**Tick**	**Tock**
When shall we	stop?	No one can	know!

Let the panpipes player add a tune when you have the two rhythms moving together.

Bring All Your Friends Together

You can have a band of your own with your pipes and box harp and rhythm instruments. Take turns being the leader with your instrument. Begin with a rhythm. Begin with a tune. Let the other players join in rhythm with you. You can play music together.

JOHN HAWKINSON and MARTHA FAULHABER

Children are naturally creative, John Hawkinson believes, and this creativity grows as children learn techniques for using art and craft materials. To put theory into practice, John Hawkinson has written and illustrated books that show how to work with water colors, pastels, and nature materials. When girls and boys see how they can use art and craft media, they freely supply their own original ideas and viewpoints.

Wondering if this same approach could be used for music, John Hawkinson went to Martha Faulhaber to discuss his ideas. Mrs. Faulhaber, who has graduate and undergraduate degrees in music, is a professional pianist and teacher. She teaches privately, but she has also had classroom experience. She has worked in the Head Start program and has taught at Dr. Bruno Bettelheim's Orthogenic School at the University of Chicago. She has studied in France and in this country under the pianist Rudolph Ganz. Electronic music and modern music theory are two fields in which Mrs. Faulhaber is studying at DePaul University, Chicago.

Always working out their ideas with children, Mr. Hawkinson and Mrs. Faulhaber began writing the kind of book they hoped would embody a free, experimental introduction to music. The result has been an exciting project that has led to two books and to tape recordings and films. While Mrs. Faulhaber has contributed theory and basic musical concepts, Mr. Hawkinson has worked out the construction details for the musical instruments and created illustrations for each activity. Two books, one for young children four or five to eight years of age, and another for older girls and boys make the *Musical Involvement Series.* Through these books the authors hope music will become a lively, provocative art any child can experience for himself.